NEW TESTAMENT CHURCH BASICS

Understanding Local Assembly
Character and Purpose

NEW TESTAMENT CHURCH BASICS

Understanding Local Assembly
Character and Purpose

by
Michael J. Penfold

JOHN RITCHIE LTD
CHRISTIAN PUBLICATIONS

40 Beansburn, Kilmarnock, Scotland

ISBN-13: 978 1 912522 29 3

40 Beansburn, Kilmarnock KA3 1RL, Scotland
Telephone: 01563 536394, Email: sales@johnritchie.co.uk.

www.ritchiechristianmedia.co.uk

Typeset by John Ritchie Ltd., Kilmarnock
Printed by Bell & Bain Ltd., Glasgow

Contents

Foreword

Truth is always under attack. The closing years of the 20th Century and the early years of the 21st have seen an unprecedented attack on the distinctive character of the local assembly, the church of God. In eight carefully-crafted and scripturally-based chapters, Michael Penfold has addressed not only the nature of the attacks, but the biblical basis for assembly practices themselves.

The importance of doctrine is stressed in his initial chapter, laying a firm foundation for all that follows. In a society marked by 'tolerance' and the rejection of 'absolute truth' in any sphere, it is difficult to overemphasise the importance of our adherence to doctrine in all that we do. Those who label assembly practice as mere 'tradition' will do well to read this chapter with care.

The purpose of the local assembly's very existence, the pattern for its design, the principles which guide it, and the practices which mark it are all detailed and shown to have a biblical basis.

Careful distinction is made between the Lord's omnipresence and His approving presence, defusing the argument raised by many that the Lord is everywhere and that therefore none can claim His presence in some unique manner. Chapters dealing with the authority which is present in a local assembly are very helpful. Mr. Penfold makes it abundantly clear that while men in leadership administer authority, its source is the Lord and His Word.

Responsibility for shepherd care and for mutual care one of another

7

is highlighted in a chapter which discusses the assembly as a haven for the care of believers. It is reminiscent of the 'inn' to which the Samaritan brought the injured traveller. All his needs were met; this is an often forgotten function of a local assembly.

One of the features occurring in many assemblies is the jettisoning of the weekly gospel meeting and of series of gospel meetings, and either replacing it with small group discussions, or abandoning it altogether. The chapter which deals with the responsibility of the assembly to be involved in the 'heralding' of the gospel should be mandatory reading for all.

The sad history of Scripture and of real-life experience has been that with the passing of time there is also a movement away from first principles. The convictions of the fathers become conveniences for the sons; what was a convenience for the sons sadly becomes compromise to the succeeding generation. A clear apostolic-call to return to first principles, to scriptural teaching concerning the assembly – not to the practices of 'early brethren' or to 'brethrenism' – is crucial.

For assembly testimony to continue in its pristine and God-honouring character we must heed the kind of warnings and words contained in this book. May they enhance the value of assembly order to those who love it; may they stir the consciences of those who merely continue out of habit; and may they restore any who have compromised the truth, having bowed to society and religion's siren call to conformity.

A. J. Higgins
Author, editor of *Truth and Tidings* magazine
February 2018

Introduction

It is common nowadays to 'choose a church' based on personal preference. If the kids' programme is 'cool', the Pastor is easy to listen to and the band is trendy, what more could one want? However, in light of the fact that the Bible contains several epistles that give *detailed doctrinal instructions* about the function, character and purpose of a local assembly[1], a 'choice of church' must of necessity involve spiritual convictions and an intelligent commitment to biblical doctrine.

This should come as no surprise. Biblical Christianity has never been about personal preferences. At its most basic level, Christianity means "God reveals His truth and I obey it". When the first local assembly was formed in Jerusalem, its members *"continued steadfastly in the apostles' doctrine"*, not *"in their own personal preferences"* (Acts 2:42). That doctrine, now enshrined in all its fulness in the New Testament, includes not only all we need to know about our Lord and Saviour, about the gospel of our salvation, about walking by faith, and about the coming Kingdom, but also about the whole spectrum of *local assembly principles and practices*.

Doctrine matters to serious Christians. The history books are full of examples of faithful believers through the ages who, often at great cost to themselves, took a stand for Bible truth. Though the simplicity of assembly order and the purity of assembly principles were, for the most part, buried for centuries under the liturgy, ceremonies and rituals of Christendom, when the Bible was translated into English (and the mother tongues of many other nations), believers' eyes were opened. They saw through the extra-Biblical ecclesiastical traditions of men and earnestly desired to get back to the simplicity of New Testament doctrine, both as to the way of salvation and also as to church doctrine and practice.

How things have changed! In the 21st Century it is not purity of doctrine that church-goers want – they don't seem to want doctrine at all! They want a church free from doctrine. No doctrine, no demands and no duties. "Let's just have a fun time, avoid debates about 'non-essentials', and not judge anyone or anything" – an attitude that is very far removed from the emphasis in the New Testament:

"Till I come, *give attendance* to reading, to exhortation, *to doctrine*" (1 Tim 4:13)
"*Take heed* unto thyself, and unto *the doctrine*" (1 Tim 4:16)
"*All scripture* is given by inspiration of God, and *is profitable for doctrine...*" (2 Tim 3:16)

So, *doctrine matters*; and in the realm of 'assembly truth', no less than in any other area of divine revelation, it is vital that we get a clear grasp of the basics. This will help us to form our own settled understanding of first principles. So, here are 8 basic purposes of a local assembly:

1. It exists for divine glory
2. It manifests the divine presence
3. It exhibits divine design
4. It administers divine authority
5. It displays divine order
6. It provides divine care
7. It proclaims divine truth
8. It fulfils the divine commission

In eight consecutive chapters, we will look at these foundational issues. These chapters first appeared as eight articles in the 'Believer's

Magazine', from April to November 2017. They have been edited and expanded slightly now that they have been combined into a whole for publication.

---

[1] The word 'assembly' rather than 'church' will be used throughout, as it more accurately expresses the meaning of the original Greek word *ekklesia*.

1

The Local Assembly Exists for Divine Glory

21st Century Western culture is, by and large, self-centred. The one-time Hilton Hotel motto, "Welcome to a world that revolves around you", neatly sums up our present age's spirit of entitlement and self-gratification. By contrast, a local assembly exists first and foremost for God – for His glory! It is not about me, my comfort or my schedule. It is about Him. It is not my assembly, or even the leadership's assembly – it is God's assembly! The Bible describes it as "the flock *of God*" (1 Pet 5:2), "the temple *of God*" (1 Cor 3:17), and *God's* husbandry or tilled field (1 Cor 3:9). We will see in later chapters that God both dwells in the assembly and rules in the assembly; but, for now, let us simply be reminded that God *owns the assembly*. It is His – and it exists for Him and to glorify Him.

Think of it this way: Creation – the Universe and everything in it – exists "in Christ, through Christ and for Christ" (Col 1:16). The Lord is simultaneously creation's architect, builder and owner. The same is true of a local assembly.

First, the local assembly exists "in Him". Writing to the assembly in Thessalonica (in ancient Greece) Paul addressed them as follows: "Unto church of the Thessalonians which is *in God the Father and in the Lord Jesus Christ*" (1 Thess 1:1). That is quite a statement. Each local assembly exists in the sphere and power of God and of Christ!

Second, the local assembly exists "through Him". There would be no assemblies without the instrumentality of the Lord Jesus. That is the idea in Acts 20:28 where it speaks of "the church of God [in Ephesus], which He hath purchased with His own blood". How costly a gathered company of Christians is! It is composed of redeemed sinners, each one the fruit of the atoning sufferings of Christ. Every local testimony exists through His cross work and through His working in salvation in localities all around the globe. That is why each assembly belongs to Him!

Third, the local assembly exists "for Him". When God asked Moses to construct a house for Him at the time of the exodus from Egypt (1,500 BC), He said, "Let them make Me a sanctuary" (Exod 25:8). The Tabernacle, and the later Temple, existed for God! And so it is today. The assembly is a "house for God". It exists to glorify Him! How precious this is! In this "present evil world" (Gal 1:4) that rejects Christ, there are assemblies dotted all around the world that exist "for Him".

Think of what glory is brought to God as companies of redeemed sinners – priests who are able to offer up spiritual sacrifices (1 Pet 2:5) – meet together weekly to "remember the Lord" at the Lord's Supper, to proclaim His death, and lift up their voices in praise, thanksgiving and worship to God for His worthy Son, the Lord Jesus (Acts 20:7, 1 Cor 11:23-26, 14:15-17). The corporate worship and praise of a local assembly renders to God the glory due to His name! This is the highest privilege and loftiest occupation of an assembly. But let us remember that *everything about an assembly* – all of its meetings, activities, order and design – has God's glory in view (1 Cor 10:31). We shall see this ever more clearly as we work our way through the chapters to come.

If the local assembly exists "in HIM, through HIM and for HIM", our first consideration cannot be "Are we attractive to the world?", or "Are we coming across as exciting to the youth of today?", or "Are we impressing the business professionals among us?". Everything must be gauged as to whether it is acceptable and well-pleasing *to the Lord*. That said, the quality and condition of our gospel literature, or hymn books, or buildings, should not give anyone a valid reason to think we are neglectful or that we do not take Christianity seriously. There is no excuse for laziness, coldness or carelessness in assembly testimony. But the modern trend of borrowing from the business world, from the rock music scene and from the celebrity culture around us, in order to attract bigger crowds and to be 'successful', is a fundamental misunderstanding of why an assembly exists. It exists not for the eye of men, but for the eye of God. We need not expect the ungodly to be impressed with what is spiritual and scriptural, unless of course the Spirit of God is working in their hearts and they are seeking God. It has been rightly said that the church the world likes best is the one that God abhors. Lost people, with their ungodly ways of thinking, impressed as they are with power, prestige and grandeur, will not find a company of pilgrims gathered to the name of Christ "outside the camp" (Heb 13:13) appealing or attractive.

So, if our culture "doesn't do group singing anymore", that should not affect our determination to follow the Bible's exhortation to assemblies to "Let the word of Christ dwell in you richly in all wisdom; teaching and admonishing one another in psalms and hymns and spiritual songs, singing with grace in your hearts to the Lord" (Col 3:16). If our culture says it no longer finds public preaching "the best way to absorb information", and would rather the emphasis was placed on multimedia, music and mime, that should not sway us from our duty to "proclaim the Word as a herald". God has clearly outlined that 'public preaching' is the chosen method for the spreading of the gospel and the teaching of the Word (1 Cor 1:17-2:5). All of this must be understood and settled in our hearts, or we will be forever chasing the latest fad in Christendom in an attempt to make the assembly look 'cool' in the eyes of the world, rather than starting from the premise "What saith the Lord?".

The fact that the assembly exists for God's glory not only reorients our thinking about who the assembly is for, but also *dignifies and elevates our service in connection with it*. If the assembly exists for God's glory, then the mid-week prayer meeting is significant and worth attending. All of the assembly's meetings and activities are of interest to heaven. In a results-orientated pragmatic society, it needs to be remembered that Sunday School work, gospel literature distribution, open air preaching, and series of gospel meetings are all primarily conducted with a view to the Lord's glory – and He is honoured and pleased with such service, whether or not it "produces results" (2 Cor 2:14-17).

As we revisit the basics of assembly testimony, there could scarcely be a more fundamental and important truth than this – *the local assembly exists for the glory of God.*

2

The Local Assembly Manifests the Divine Presence

Our thoughts now turn to a second fundamental purpose of a local assembly – it manifests the presence of God.

Since the beginning of creation it has always been God's purpose to dwell among His people. Adam and Eve heard God's voice, knew His presence and enjoyed fellowship with Him in Eden's garden. Later, in the book of Genesis, Jacob met God in "Bethel" (Hebrew: "house of God") and exclaimed, "Surely *the LORD is in this place*...this is none other but *the house of God*, and this is the gate of heaven" (Gen 28:16-17). Again, no sooner had the nation of Israel been called out of Egypt, redeemed by blood and baptised unto Moses in the Red Sea, than God declared His purpose; "Let them make Me a sanctuary, *that I may dwell among them*" (Exod 25:8). Turning to the other end of the Bible, the apostle John sees the 'a new heaven and a new earth' and writes that "the tabernacle of God is with men, *and He will dwell with them*, and they shall be His people" (Rev 21:3). Suffice to say, God's presence among His people is a chief theme of Scripture.

It is important to distinguish between God's omnipresence and what we might call His "manifested presence". The fact that the Lord is "present everywhere" does not hinder Him from manifesting His presence in a particular location at a particular time. In the Tabernacle of Moses the Lord dwelt "between the cherubim" (Exod 25:22). Again, the "glory of the Lord" filled Solomon's temple in Jerusalem, a city which is referred to repeatedly as "the place that I have chosen to set My name" (Neh 1:9). Even in the Millennial Kingdom, Jerusalem will be called *"the Lord is there"* (Eze 48:35).

All of this invites the question, "Where does God dwell today?". The Tabernacle of Moses and the Temple of Solomon have long since perished. Is God's presence to be found in the cathedrals, shrines and basilicas of Christendom? Let the Word of God supply the answer: "For w*here* two or three are gathered together in My name, *there am I* in the midst of them" (Matt 18:20). This pivotal verse breaks down neatly into three parts, as follows:

First, "Where Two or Three are Gathered Together"

Note that Matthew 18:20 is not saying "Where two or three people *decide to get together*, there am I." The verb "gathered together" is in the passive voice, which means the "two or three" *have been gathered together by God.*[1] Exactly how does God gather His people together today so that He may dwell among them? Come with me for a moment back to Ancient Greece, a culture that featured 'town criers' who heralded local announcements in the public square. The Greek word for a town crier or herald is *kerux*. When political or legislative matters needed to be settled in a Greek town or city, the *kerux* stood in the street and loudly called the civilians together. Once the *kerux* had announced the call, out the people came from their homes and businesses and gathered together in a group. This group, this "called-out company", was called an *ekklesia* (from *ek*/out and *kaleo*/to call).[2]

Have you got the picture? A *kerux* issued the call, and an *ekklesia* was formed. Now, the Bible uses these two words – *kerux* and *ekklesia* – in a spiritual sense. The apostle Paul called himself a *kerux* in 2 Timothy 1:11. He said, "I am appointed *a preacher*". The New Testament concept of preaching is that of a herald who publicly announces the message of the gospel. As for the word *ekklesia*, this is the regular New Testament word for 'church' or 'assembly'. An assembly is neither a building, nor a denomination, nor an order of men. It is a "called-out company". How is it called out? - by the Lord through the gospel preacher (the *kerux*). Why is it called out? In order to be "gathered together" to the name of the Lord Jesus – and that is where the Lord dwells today! When sinners respond to the gospel call in repentance and faith, are baptised, and are gathered in a local called-out company "to His name", God makes them His dwelling.

It should be noted that the verb "gathered together" in Matthew 18:20 is a perfect participle, which means it describes something that both *has* happened and *is still* happening. It emphasises 'state', not something passing or temporary. This gathered company has a history! Literally translated, the verse should read: "Where two or three are, having been and being gathered together in My name, there am I". An assembly gathering is not a haphazard, *ad hoc*, social get together – but a settled spiritual gathering together.

Second, "In My name"

The formula "into the name" – using the Greek preposition *eis* – occurs in three different connections in the New Testament, each of which is filled with significance:

1. Salvation - "Believe on [*eis*] His name" (John 1:12, 2:23, 3:18)
2. Baptism - "Baptising them in [*eis*] the name" (Matt 28:19, Acts 8:16, 19:5)
3. Gathering - "Gathered together in [*eis*] My name" (Matt 18:20)

These three steps match what we later read in Acts 2 where people were 1. saved, 2. baptised, and 3. added to the assembly in Jerusalem.

What does being "gathered in His name" actually mean? Let me suggest two leading thoughts: 'association' and 'authority'.

1. Association

An assembly is not gathered to a doctrine, or to a figure of Church history, or to a human organisation. An assembly gathers "into His name". Gathering in or to the Lord's name means *coming into association with a Person* – the Lord Jesus Christ. Since in the Bible someone's name speaks of their character, "gathering in Christ's name" means associating with His character – His truth, His holiness and His majesty. This has solemn consequences.

A vital New Testament passage – 2 Corinthians 6:14-18 – outlines the theology behind the great truth of "separation". Note carefully the wording: "*I will dwell in them*, and walk in them; and I will be their God, and they shall be My people, *wherefore* come out from among them, and be ye separate saith the Lord." Notice the word "wherefore". Why should Christians be separate from all that is contrary to righteousness, light and truth? *Because the Lord is present among them and they are thus associated with His name!*

When Paul the apostle visited Corinth, he encountered a wicked city steeped in immorality and idolatry. God moved mightily through gospel preaching and an assembly of God was planted in the midst of that city. The Lord dwelt among His people in *Corinth!* That involved far-reaching consequences for the converted Corinthians. Because of the Lord's presence among them and *their association with Him,* they had to sever their associations with the culture of Corinth. They learned that they could not partake of "the table of demons" in the pagan temple at the same time as partaking of "the table of the Lord" in the assembly (1 Cor 10:21). They learned that a local assembly must reflect the holiness of the One who dwells in it. Paul warned the Corinthian believers: "The [inner] temple of God is holy, which temple ye are" (1 Cor 3:17). To be part of an assembly where God dwells necessitates that we separate from the unrighteousness and godlessness of the political, religious and social "present evil world" around us – including its drinking houses, its movie and music industries, and its idolatrous sports-mad culture.

2. Authority

A 'name' can also function as a substitute word (a metonym) for authority. If a soldier knocks at your door and demands "Open up in the name of the King", he is not referring to the appellation "George" or "Henry" or "William"! He means "Open up in the authority of the King". Gathering "in the Lord's name" means "coming under and acknowledging His authority". This is crucial. The "Lord in the midst" carries not just the idea of "God dwelling" but also of "God ruling", and only where believers "gather in His name", thus owning His authority and Lordship, is the presence of Christ known corporately.

Third, "There Am I in the Midst of Them"

The import of this statement is staggering. The One who inhabits eternity, of whom Solomon said "Who is able to build Him an house, seeing the heaven and heaven of heavens cannot contain him?" (2 Chron 2:6), now dwells among those who are simply "gathered in His name". To be part of a local assembly thus gathered is a greater privilege than being a member of the House of Commons, or of the House of Bishops, or indeed a member of any club, guild, association or body, no matter how prestigious or powerful it may be thought to be by men. No high ecclesiastical sanction is required; no Papal decree; no denominational affiliation. What a discovery! What a privilege!

[1.] Although the Matthew 18 passage initially concerns assembly discipline, by verse 20 a general principle is being given.

[2.] The "lawful assembly" mentioned by the town clerk in Ephesus in Acts 19:39 is one such secular use of the word *ekklesia*.

3

The Local Assembly Exhibits Divine Design

We have seen that the Lord both owns the assembly and dwells in the assembly. Let us now consider the fact that *He designed the assembly* and that its order, structure and character showcase His wisdom. These three facts are placed side by side, in picture form, in Israel's history in Exodus 25:8-9:

1. **Ownership** "Let them make Me a sanctuary"
2. **Residency** "That I may dwell among them"
3. **Design** "According to all that I show thee, after the pattern"

God's house in the *Old Testament* had a pattern. With painstaking precision God specified the Tabernacle's materials, dimensions, layout and its method of construction. Nothing was left to human imagination. God said to Moses, "See…that thou make all things *according to the pattern* showed to thee" (Heb 8:5).[1] This pattern served to reveal God's wisdom and glory.

Is there a pattern for God's dwelling today? Yes! We are not left to just make it up as we go along. The New Testament *gives a definite pattern and blueprint to be followed in all cultures, on all continents and throughout all centuries of the present dispensation.*

For example, in 1 Corinthians 3 we learn *how to build* into the assembly, while in 1 Timothy 3 we are told *how to behave* in the assembly. Note the terms Paul uses in 1 Corinthians 3. As the preacher who brought the gospel to Corinth and saw the assembly planted, he calls himself a "wise *master builder*" who laid the "*foundation*" for "*God's building*". He designates the assembly "the *inner temple* of God" and speaks of materials of "*gold, silver and precious stones*". The deliberate metaphorical parallels with the Temple of old could hardly be clearer.

If Moses and Solomon were duty bound to follow the Divine Architect's plans for God's house in a past era, what about us now? Note carefully Paul's words in relation to the local assembly; "...let every man take heed *how he buildeth*" (1 Cor 3:10). Why the need for care in *how* a local assembly is built? *Because how faithful we are to the divine blueprint will be assessed when we meet the Lord in heaven* (1 Cor 3:10-15). The Lord will hold us accountable in these matters because He has outlined in the New Testament clear, detailed and definite instructions for us to follow.

The Wisdom of God or the Wisdom of Men?

Throughout the ages, human nature has repeatedly displayed a tendency to think it knows better than the Divine Designer. The sons of Aaron introduced 'strange fire'. Ahaz introduced a foreign altar. David introduced a new cart. This weakness has continued into the present age. In the assembly at Corinth the believers were *not building correctly* – they were working according to man's wisdom, not God's. Though, in the wisdom of God, Paul and Apollos were to be seen as simply 'servants', the Corinthians had put them on a pedestal and turned them into 'celebrity speakers'. They had elevated gift over spirituality, knowledge over love, outward performance over inward grace, and the greatness of men over the 'foolishness of the cross'. So, Paul wrote 1 Corinthians to explain the difference between worldly wisdom and the wisdom of God not only in relation to the gospel (Ch 1) and the communication of truth (Ch 2), but also in relation to "how to build" local assemblies (Ch 3).

The use of human wisdom in building local assemblies did not die out with the Corinthians! In our generation, for example, the pressure to look appealing to the world has resulted in a wholesale jettisoning of any thought of strictly following a 'New Testament pattern', and a turning instead to 'what works' ("the end justifies the means"). Exposition has been surrendered to entertainment, preaching to performance, doctrine to drama and theology to theatrics. The emphasis in many places is now simply on big numbers, big names, and big sounds. But for Paul the choice was simple. Build according to man's wisdom – and at the Judgment Seat, all will be seen as worthless; or build according to God's wisdom – and one's work will abide (1 Cor 3:9-15).

Optional or Mandatory?

It is well to remember that the pattern for a New Testament assembly is mandatory, not optional. New Testament assembly principles such as gathering to the name of the Lord Jesus alone, the distinction in roles between male and female in relation to teaching and leadership, the acknowledgement of headship by the symbols of the covered and uncovered head, the plurality of elders, the weekly Lord's Supper on the Lord's Day – these are all non-negotiable features of the pattern. They form part of "the apostles' doctrine" in which we are to "continue steadfastly" (Acts 2:42).

Take the issue of elders, or "church leadership", to coin a phrase. In the Anglican Communion, one Bishop is appointed and exercises authority over hundreds of churches. Is this according to the pattern? No. This is the polar opposite of the pattern. Biblical assembly leadership is not "one bishop over many assemblies" but "many bishops (overseers) in one assembly" (Acts 14:23, 20:17, Jas 5:14).[2]

What of a name? Can we not take to ourselves a convenient banner such as 'Baptist' or 'Presbyterian'? No. That would be to violate the pattern. Any such name is at the same time both wider and narrower than the Biblical titles of 'Christians', 'believers', 'brethren' and 'saints'. Wider, in that denominational names include believers and unbelievers alike; narrower, and sectarian, in that they exclude all who refuse to adopt them.

25

What of women speaking in assembly meetings? Is there anything in the pattern to guide us? Yes. Paul says, "Let your women keep silence in the churches" and a few verses later states: "The things I write to you are *the commandments of the Lord*" (1 Cor 14:34-37). Note the word 'commandments'. The Bible's teaching on this issue is not a suggestion! Yet human wisdom will always seek to circumvent the pattern. Would it not liven up our prayer meetings if the sisters could take part? Could we not have the men praying in one room and the women in the other? What about having a "women's conference" where sisters can teach, so long as men are not present? Yet nothing of this is found in the New Testament. Neither by direct commandment, nor by example, nor based on any general principle can we find assembly meetings broken down into 'small groups', men's retreats, women's conferences or youth conferences. Quite the reverse – in His wisdom and for His glory, as well as for our protection and blessing, God has designed all the meetings of an assembly to be open to all the believers, to be overseen by local elders, with the truth of headship symbolically on display, and all the teaching carried out by gifted men.

A Fitting Design for the Present Dispensation

God knows best. His design for the local assembly not only reveals His wisdom, but also reflects the character of the present dispensation. Because the types and shadows of the Old Covenant have found their fulfilment in Christ, Christians today have no need for naves and chancels, for choirs and vestments, or for feasts and festivals, all of which hark back to these obsolete foreshadowings. Our calling is to gather to His name alone, a remnant testimony outside of the political, social and religious camps of this present evil world. Jew and Gentile in fellowship together, worshipping God in spirit and in truth, and displaying the divine order of headship to angels – thus reversing the chaos of Eden's garden and delighting the heart of God in the midst of a godless rebellious culture.

When considering the difficult questions of our day in relation to assembly order and practice, the words of C.H. Mackintosh are weighty and thought-provoking:

"In the presence of the searcher of hearts, ask yourself this plain, pointed question, 'Am I sanctioning by my presence, or adopting in my practice, any departure from, or neglect of, the Word of God?' Make this a solemn, personal matter before the Lord. Be assured of it; it is of the very deepest moment, the very last importance. If you find that you have been, in any wise, connected with, or involved in, *ought that wears not the distinct stamp of divine sanction,* reject it at once and for ever. Yes, reject it, though arrayed in the imposing vestments of antiquity, accredited by the voice of tradition, and putting forward the almost irresistible plea of expediency. If you cannot say, in reference to everything with which you stand connected, 'this is the thing which the Lord hath commanded', then away with it unhesitatingly, away with it for ever."

In light of the day of review at the Judgment Seat, our first thought in building must be faithfulness to revealed truth (1 Cor 4:2). Let us be careful what doctrine we teach and what practices we encourage; let us take heed "how we build".

---

[1] Likewise for Solomon's Temple (1 Chron 28:12).

[2] An elder and an overseer (translated "bishop" in the KJV), are two titles for the same person. See Acts 20:17-28, Titus 1:5-7 and 1 Peter 5:1-2. 'Elder' indicates maturity; 'overseer' indicates work.

4

The Local Assembly Administers Divine Authority

In previous chapters we have examined a number of basic truths about the local assembly. First, the Lord *owns* it. Second, He *dwells* in it. Third, He *designed* it. Now we come to a fourth fundamental consideration – He *rules* it. The Bible teaches that *Christ is the Lord of the assembly!* Local companies of God's people are to own Him as sovereign, bow to His authority, and give Him the pre-eminence in all things. In a lawless, chaotic and rebellious world, the local assembly is presently the only sphere on earth where divine rule and authority are corporately acknowledged and where God's Word and will are supreme. What a privilege to be called to honour the Lord in this unique way!

Authority Identified

As Christians in a locality "gather to His name" they collectively come under the lordship of Christ and are responsible to Him alone as their sovereign Lord. The great 'local assembly epistle' of the New Testament – 1 Corinthians – regularly highlights this truth. It tells us that the spiritual gifts used in the assembly are given by *"the Lord"* (1 Cor 3:5); that assembly discipline is carried out in the name of the *"Lord* Jesus Christ" (1 Cor 5:4); that the breaking of bread is "the *Lord's* supper" (1 Cor 11:20); that the Bible's instructions about who should participate and how and when, are "the commandments of *the Lord"* (1 Cor 14:37); and that the activity of the assembly is "the work of *the Lord"* (1 Cor 15:58).

Such is the Lord's authority over each assembly that He will even at times intervene *directly* to maintain its order and holiness. The Bible warns, "If any man defile the temple of God, him shall God destroy" (1 Cor 3:17). Examples of such divine intervention are given in 1 Corinthians 11:30: "…many are weak and sickly among you, and many sleep [have died]", and Acts 5:1-11: "…great fear came upon all the church, and upon as many as heard these things [the sudden death of Ananias and Sapphira]". It is easy for us, in our natural weakness, to become all too familiar with these matters and to forget the seriousness of our corporate assembly privileges and responsibilities; but who could read these passages without solemnly concluding that, in the words of Henry Hitchman, "…*the very last place where we can do as we like is the assembly…In it Christ is Lord and subjection to Him becomes all saints*"?[1]

Authority Acknowledged

The subject of the Lordship of Christ over the local assembly is an eminently practical doctrine – and supremely challenging to our often inconsistent and undevoted hearts! How should an assembly acknowledge the Lordship of Christ? Here are some pointers:

- By rendering loving, obedient service to Him (Eph 5:19, Phil 2:17)
- By reverent behaviour in assembly gatherings (1 Cor 11:20-34)
- By giving respect to the assembly's elders (Heb 13:17)
- By elders not acting as 'lords' who only desire pre-eminence (3 John 9)
- By public teaching being given only by those who are divinely gifted (Acts 13:1)
- By gifted brethren working harmoniously for the edification of the saints (1 Cor 14:29-33).
- By the exercise of brotherly love instead of envy, bitterness and anger (Eph 4:31-32)
- By not leaving serious moral or doctrinal evil to remain unjudged in the assembly (1 Cor 5:1-13, 1 Tim 1:20).

These features, actions and attitudes are indicative of submission to Christ and His Word and help us to understand what it means to be collectively under His lordship.

The lordship of Christ also impacts the topic of the design of the local assembly (see previous chapter). If *the Lord* has expressly revealed His will – in His Word – as to how an assembly should be structured, ordered and led, dare we alter, diminish or add to that pattern? Think of a large mansion in which resides 'the Lord of the Manor'. Because he owns and lives in the property, nothing happens without his knowledge, his approval or his blessing. Imagine then, if you will, some evening dinner party guests reconfiguring the layout of the drawing room without his express permission – unthinkable! Likewise, because Christ is Lord in the assembly, may He graciously preserve us from introducing anything inconsistent with His lordship.

But without a Church Council, a Creed or a Confession, how can we know what the Lord requires of us as we gather in His name? Through His Word, the Bible! *If Christ is the assembly's Lord, then His Word is its absolute standard.* When Paul said farewell to the elders of the assembly in Ephesus for the last time, he said "I commend you *to God and to the Word of His grace*" (Acts 20:39). Even though Paul knew that false teachers were soon to cause havoc in Ephesus, he left the elders with nothing but "God and His Word". What a powerful reminder of the sufficiency of God's authoritative Word for all the assembly's needs!

Authority Administered

But what is to be done when serious doctrinal or moral evil rears its ugly head in the local assembly? How should such cases be handled? What authority has the assembly to act in judgment?

God has given human beings the right to exercise discipline in a number of spheres. For example, governments are given authority from God to

31

punish evildoers (Rom 13:1-5). Again, parents are authorised to administer chastisement to their children (Prov 23:13-14). What is true in government and in the home holds true in the local assembly too. It is authorised by the Lord to act in discipline when evil needs to be purged, for the preservation of the testimony and the honour of His name.

This is a sobering truth. Assemblies of God are tasked with administering the authority of God in cases requiring excommunication. In so doing they are carrying out God's will on earth. When a certain brother in the church of God at Corinth was put out of fellowship for sexual immorality, Paul the apostle spoke of the excommunication being done as the assembly gathered "in the name [authority] of the Lord Jesus Christ" and "with the power of our Lord Jesus Christ" (1 Cor 5:4).

In Matthew 18 there is a description of an assembly disciplinary process in which the assembly's action is described in terms of "binding and loosing". Verse 18 says, "Verily I say unto you, Whatsoever ye shall bind on earth shall be bound in heaven: and whatsoever ye shall loose on earth shall be loosed in heaven". To grasp what is being said here, it is helpful to note that the verbs "shall be bound" and "shall be loosed" are both perfect passive participles. Young's *Literal Translation* gives the sense as follows: "Whatever things ye may bind upon the earth shall be having been bound in the heavens, and whatever things ye may loose on the earth shall be having been loosed in the heavens." The verse is not saying that the act of excommunication carried out on earth is subsequently ratified by God in heaven. Quite the reverse. Heaven binds first; then the assembly binds on earth what has already been bound above.

To put it in plain language, when a believer is put out of fellowship, that excommunication is the binding of a disciplinary action on earth that reflects God's verdict already given in heaven. And, if the believer later repents and is restored to fellowship, the binding action is loosed, again in accordance with heaven's will. Thus do Millennial conditions – "Thy will be done in earth, as it is in heaven" – find their answer in the present age!

F.W. Grant says of this passage, "[The assembly] *is not a democracy, but a monarchy most absolute…The church is a body not legislative but executive: it does not decree what shall be, but decides upon what is. It has authority to act, but upon lines laid down for it.*"[2] That is to say, the assembly does not function like a Parliament that develops and passes new laws. An assembly simply administers established divine scriptural principles in fellowship with heaven. In the words of W.E. Vine, "An act of church discipline is not simply the act of the assembly; when rightly used it is the exercise of the authority of Christ, carried out in His name and power."[3]

This vital subject of 'authority and the assembly' can now be summarised in three points:

* In the authority of the Lord it gathers (Matt 18:20)
* To the authority of the Lord it submits (1 Cor 3:5, 14:37)
* By the authority of the Lord it acts (Matt 18:18, 1 Cor 5:4)

This concludes our look at authority in terms of lordship. In the next chapter, we will consider authority in terms of headship.

[1.] H. Hitchman, *Some Scriptural Principles of the Christian Assembly* (Glasgow, Gospel Tract Publications 1988), p. 74

[2.] F.W. Grant, *The Numerical Bible, The Gospels* (New York: Loizeaux Bros. 1897), p. 186-187

[3.] W.E. Vine, *Collected Writings, Vol 5*, (Glasgow: Gospel Tract Publications 1985), p. 174.

5

The Local Assembly Displays
Divine Order

We take our leave of the subject of 'lordship' to look now at 'headship'. These two topics – both of which significantly impact assembly life and testimony – need to be carefully distinguished. Lordship has to do with rule; headship with role. Lordship emphasises supremacy and sovereignty; headship emphasises function and office. Lordship means that God has absolute rights over men and women equally; headship that He has different roles for men and women administratively.

The Bible says that God is the head of Christ, but never "God is the Lord of Christ" (1 Cor 11:3). Why? – because, though Christ is administratively subject to God as to His role and function, He remains essentially equal to God in His nature and being. Similarly, men and women are essentially equal, but have different roles in divine order – man as head, woman as helper. So, though the man is the head of the woman, he is not the woman's lord. Headship is not the power of a superior over an inferior. To be someone's head is to be in a position of authority over them and of responsibility for them, though they may be one's equal essentially.

Properly understood, Satan's first attack in the Bible – in Eden – was an attack on the order of headship. Yes, Satan wanted our first parents to rebel and disobey their Creator, but the way in which he went about it showed he was also intent on undermining and overturning divine order in the process. He approached the woman, Eve, and lured her into taking the lead in the first transgression (Gen 3:1, 1 Tim 2:14). In the words of J Allen, "...Eve stepped out of her place; in so doing she overturned a divine order and Adam, with eyes open, accepted her leadership with disastrous results. Both thus violated their God-given status; Eve by an assumption of authority or dominion she did not rightly possess, and Adam, in a renunciation of authority he had no right to make".[1]

For His own glory, for the preservation of His people and for the eye of angels (1 Cor 11:10), God desires Eden's chaos to be reversed in the local assembly, as divine order is accepted and acknowledged – both literally and symbolically.

Literal Acknowledgment

Headship is demonstrated in the local assembly as men take responsibility in leadership and participation as head, while sisters submit to that lead in their role as helper. In 1 Timothy 2 Paul speaks of the issue of authority and male headship, stating "I will therefore that the men [the males] pray in every place" (v. 8, JND), and then outlines the numerous ways in which sisters, as helpers, fulfil their role alongside the brothers; by their godly dress and deportment; by their good works; by their submissive silence and by their godly faithful role in the home. So, in the local assembly, the glory of men as head is seen in their speaking and leading, while the glory of women is seen in these aspects of their role as helpers.

In our day of egalitarianism and feminism it is vital to understand *the reason why* women are not allowed "to teach nor to exercise authority over man" (1 Tim 2:12, JND). It is not because they are inferior, nor is it a punishment for being deceived in the garden of Eden. Adam's guilt in Eden was actually greater than Eve's, due to his status as head. *It is simply because of the original order of headship in creation.* "Adam was first formed, then Eve" (v. 13). In other words, the original plan and design of God, before sin entered into the world, was that Adam should take the lead as head, while Eve fulfilled the role of supporter and helper.[2] And, argues

Paul, what went wrong in Eden, on both Adam and Eve's part, is to be corrected in the assembly. Men are not to sit passively and silently, never praying or participating in any way; and women are not to speak out on their own, because public prayer and preaching are both representative acts of leadership, not becoming of their role in the order of headship.

Symbolic Acknowledgment

Headship is also to be demonstrated symbolically. How? – by men having uncovered heads and women wearing head coverings in assembly gatherings. Sisters wear head coverings for exactly the same reason as they keep silence – *because of the order of creation;* "Neither was the man created for the woman, but the woman for the man. *For this cause* ought the woman to have power [the symbol of authority] on her head" (1 Cor 11:9-10). As a woman puts on a head covering she is saying, "I am here to help, but I am under authority". Likewise, a brother with an uncovered head is saying, "I am here to take my role of godly responsible leadership in participation and teaching." Notice that 1 Cor 11:10 calls a head covering a "symbol of authority". A.T. Robertson explains: "The veil on the woman's head is the symbol of the authority that the man with the uncovered head has over her".[3] So, if a sister refuses to wear a head covering she is saying, "I reject the authority of man". Effectively she is saying "I want to be the man". Thus she dishonours man – her head – and rejects her role in God's order. Likewise if a man puts a head covering on, he is saying "I am not under Christ; I am under the woman". Thus he dishonours his head – Christ – by refusing to take his proper place in the order of headship.

1 Corinthians 11:7 says man is "the image and glory of God". The way the words 'image' and 'glory' are joined here by 'and', means this phrase can be translated "man is the majestic image of God". That is, in Eden man's function was to represent God as His vice-regent on earth. Eve, his wife, fulfilled a supporting role. She was created "for the man". However, note that, when describing the woman, Paul simply says she is "the glory of the man", not his image. Why? – because while man represents God,

the woman does not represent man – she complements man. She is the "glory of man" in the same sense that the Eiffel Tower is "the glory of Paris" – it enhances Paris and adds to its majesty and renown. In the case of a husband and wife we read in Proverbs 12:4, "A virtuous woman is a crown to her husband". So, in the assembly, as the sisters – married and single – cover their heads and give submissive help, support and service, they function in their God-given role as "the glory of the man". Stephen Hulshizer helpfully summarises the teaching: "The man demonstrates, by his uncovered head…that he…is to lovingly lead in willing submission to his spiritual head, Christ. The woman demonstrates, by her covered head…that she willingly submits to his spiritual leadership".[4]

Gender Distinction

Even when the assembly is not gathered, there is a natural every day way in which God's order of headship for men and women is to be displayed – by short hair on men and long hair on women (1 Cor 11:14-15). J.N. Darby helpfully states, "…a woman's [long] hair, her glory and ornament, showed, in contrast with the hair of man, that she was not made to present herself with the boldness of man before all. Given as a [natural] veil, her hair showed that modesty, submission…was her true position, her distinctive glory".[5]

The two subjects of hair length and head coverings are closely connected in 1 Corinthians 11. J Hunter explains: "In v. 5 the refusal to wear a covering is assumed (in the sight of God) to be equivalent to having no covering of any kind...If the long hair and the covered head of the woman set forth her recognition of the headship of the man, then the uncovered head and the cut or shorn hair declare her insubjection to the man."[6] The Bible teaches that if a woman refuses to wear the spiritual sign (the head covering), she might as well take off the natural sign as well (her long hair), because the head covering is, in the assembly, what the long hair is in nature – a sign of submission. And these two signs of submission complement each other; the woman's long hair is given to her as a natural covering "answering to"

(v. 15) her spiritual head covering or veil. Thus if a woman deliberately has short hair, she is being insubmissive. She is refusing to take her place in divine order by looking like a man. And, *vice versa* for a man who has long hair – "it is a shame unto him" (v. 14).

May the Lord help us to understand this vital subject and, in both the literal and symbolic acknowledgement of headship, joyfully and intelligently take up our God-given roles in accordance with revealed Scripture.

---

[1] J. Allen, *What the Bible Teaches, 1 Timothy* (Kilmarnock, John Ritchie Ltd. 1983), p. 208

[2] Gen 2:18-25, 1 Cor 11:10-16, 14:34-35, 1 Tim 5:8-15

[3] A.T. Robertson, *New Testament Word Pictures*, comments on 1 Cor 11:10

[4] S. Hulshizer, *The Truth of Headship* (York, PA, USA, Spread the Word 1992), p. 39

[5] J.N. Darby, *Synopsis, Vol 4* (Winschoten, Netherlands, H.L. Heijkoop 1970), p. 232

[6] J Hunter, *What the Bible Teaches, 1 Corinthians* (Kilmarnock, John Ritchie Ltd. 1986), p. 122-123.

6

The Local Assembly Provides Divine Care

What a place the assembly is! – where God's glory is preeminent; His presence is known; His wisdom is displayed; His rule is acknowledged, and His order of headship is honoured and displayed. We come now to a sixth purpose: the assembly is where *God's care is experienced*.

From Eden's garden all the way to the future Millennial kingdom, it has always been God's desire to care for His own. At the present time in history, *the local assembly is the place* where God intends believers to be nurtured, preserved and developed; and, where each can fulfil their *own* responsibility to "look out not only for [their] own interests, but also for the interests of others" (Phil 2:4, NKJV).[1]

In the first and second centuries AD, gathering with other believers was a high-risk activity. Yet meetings were a lifeline to persecuted believers – they wanted to be there! Why? In ancient Rome what would you have done without your fellow believers? They were the ones who fed and sheltered you when expelled from your community. They encouraged you to press on in the faith. They stood with you in the arena as the lions closed in. And so, after being arrested, interrogated and released, where did the apostles go? To their "own company" – to the Christians (Acts 4:23).

True, each believer can, without attending meetings, personally experience much of the pastoral care of the great Shepherd, the Lord Jesus. But, despite the inevitable problems that come with being around 'people', it is clearly God's mind that each believer should experience and reciprocate care in the context of a corporate company of God's people (Acts 2:41-42, Heb 10:25).

The blessing of belonging to an assembly has often been likened to "coals in a fire". A single coal that accidentally falls onto the hearth soon grows cold and dies out. Christians need each other; and not just for support. Being with other Christians who, like ourselves, are not perfect, forces us to grow and change as we constantly learn and relearn that "love covers a multitude of sins" (1 Pet 4:8).

Let us now look at four categories of local assembly care.

1. Care of the Assembly by Elders

Concerning elders Paul says, "If a man know not how to rule his own house, how shall he *take care of the church of God*?" (1 Tim 3:5). Notice the parallel between elders in an assembly and fathers in a home. Assembly leadership is clearly intended to be paternal in nature and motivated by familial love.[2]

But how should elders take care of an assembly? Their primary task is to "feed the flock".[3] Believers in local assemblies should be well fed by elders who "declare the whole counsel of God" through regular focussed Bible teaching (Acts 20:17-35). Being "apt to teach" would also enable elders to give Scripture-based personal counsel as the need arises.

There are so many other aspects of shepherd care. Elders should pray for and take an interest in all the local believers. Elders' homes should be open to all, as they and their wives are "given to hospitality". Visitation of the sick and of others, along with support of the weak and the faint-hearted, are all different aspects of the "good work" in which overseers are engaged (1 Tim 3:1, 1 Thess 5:14).

The efforts of elders to show care for the assembly as a whole may at times prove an unpopular and thankless task. The unruly and disorderly may need to be disciplined, and false teaching may need to be confronted.[4] But, though Biblical shepherding will prove severely challenging, the Lord graciously promises compensation for those who faithfully bear the burden of shepherd care in the assembly (1 Pet 5:4).

2. Care of the Assembly by "One Another"

All believers, not just elders, have a duty of care. Yes, elders are to be given to hospitality and are to support struggling saints in practical ways, but so are all believers![5] So, while the care of elders uniquely involves aspects of government and guidance, each Christian has a responsibility to care for their brothers and sisters. Assembly fellowship is not just about getting – it is about giving!

The Bible illustrates the local assembly under the metaphor of the human body. *Each and every part of the body is useful and needful.* All the various body members "care for one another". Indeed, when one part of the body is in pain, the rest of the body comes out in sympathy (1 Cor 12:25-26)! The concept of "one another" is a constant theme of the New Testament – "love one another", "edify one another", "serve one another", "bear one another's burdens" and "pray for one another".[6] And we are not just to care for our own class, culture or age group. James condemns fussing over rich Christians at the expense of the poor (Jas 2:1-9). May the Lord help us to be impartial as we care for others.

There's a 'ministry of care' for every demographic in the assembly. Care for older saints by the young starts with an attitude of respect (1 Tim 5:1-2). Care for single sisters by young men is seen in pure actions and attitudes (1 Tim 5:2). Care for young mothers by older experienced ones is given as they pass on the wisdom of their years to the next generation (Titus 2:4-5).

The fact that, in 1 Corinthians, an entire chapter about love (Ch 13) is sandwiched in between a chapter about spiritual gifts (Ch 12) and another chapter about their use in assembly gatherings (Ch 14), indicates that our fellow believers will likely care very little how much we know, unless they know how much we care. Do you have a care for the Lord's people in your home assembly?

3. Care of Visitors, New Converts and Unbelievers

Believers away on holiday or business will seek to meet up with like-minded saints wherever they go. This provides opportunities for locals to show hospitality. The Greek word for 'hospitality' basically means *love of strangers* (Heb 13:2). The Bible also highlights those occasions when "the unlearned or unbelievers" come to assembly meetings. They too should be shown care and concern - so that unlearned believers may learn, and that unbelievers may be saved. Let them see that "God is among you of a truth" (1 Cor 14:25) and take note that we are Christ's disciples because we "love one another" (John 13:35). Do you take time to be friendly to visitors?

Another needy group are new believers. In addition to the teaching and help they receive as they attend all the gatherings of the local assembly, converts with no Christian background may benefit from informal one-on-one input from experienced Christians in their homes. Remember that godly couple Aquila and Priscilla? They took Apollos into their home and taught him "the way of God more perfectly" (Acts 18:26).

4. Care of Evangelists, Teachers and Missionaries

Our final category of care relates to the needs of 'commended workers'. Those who spend all their time preaching and teaching the Word of God have a right to be supported financially (1 Cor 9:14, Gal 6:6). This responsibility falls at the feet of assemblies and the individuals in them. Jack Hunter writes: "The NT knows nothing of one-man ministry, of a man being paid a stipend or salary in return for spiritual services. The long established principle of clerisy and the more modern innovation of paid-pastors in some assemblies are foreign to the word of God. There are those gifted by the Lord to feed the flock and spread the gospel, who have gone forth 'taking nothing of the Gentiles'. It is our privilege and responsibility to support them."[7]

Challenge

The apostle Paul was daily burdened with the "anxious care of all the churches" (2 Cor 11:28). Should we not wholeheartedly care at least for the one to which we belong? There should be no 'passengers' in God's assembly; no 'Sunday morning only' Christians. May we be freshly gripped by a "purpose of heart" to do all in our power, as led and sustained by the Lord, to see the local assembly cared for and preserved! But make no mistake; as we are "one heart and one soul" with others (Acts 4:32) and are "continuing steadfastly" in fellowship with them (Acts 2:42), we will not only enjoy all the privileges of assembly fellowship but will also feel the sharp end of its weighty cares and responsibilities.

[1.] The Christian home is also a vital sphere of care, but all believers do not have this privilege.

[2.] Unlike the money-oriented hired hand who *"careth not* for the sheep" (John 10:13)

[3.] Acts 20:28, 1 Tim 3:2, 1 Pet 5:2

[4.] Titus 1:10-13, 2 Thess 3:6-15, 1 Tim 1:19-20

[5.] 1 Tim 3:2, Titus 1:8, Rom 12:13, 1 Pet 4:9, Acts 20:35, Rom 12:13

[6.] John 13:34, Rom 14:19, Gal 5:13, Gal 6:2, Jas 5:6

[7.] J Hunter, *What the Bible Teaches, Galatians* (Kilmarnock, John Ritchie Ltd. 1983), p. 97.

7

The Local Assembly Proclaims Divine Truth

Before looking, in this chapter, at the local assembly's role as a vehicle for the dissemination and defence of Bible doctrine, a particular aspect of 'proclaiming divine truth' must be mentioned.

In the weekly Lord's Supper, sometimes called "the breaking of bread" (Acts 20:7), the local assembly is given a unique privilege and responsibility. As believers corporately eat the bread and drink the cup they "proclaim the Lord's death till He comes" (1 Cor 11:26, NKJV). This is designed to be the act of an established gathered local assembly, not of individuals in their homes or hospital beds. What a high and holy privilege is here afforded to local assemblies – to proclaim, announce and make known the truth, reality and purpose of the death of Christ "until He comes"!

Bearing this very specific proclamation of divine truth in mind, we now come to the more general purpose of the assembly in relation to the truth of God as a whole.

The relationship between "*God* and truth" seems obvious to most Christians. God is the source of truth, all truth is God's truth, and without God there can be no truth. The concept of "*the Bible* and truth" is also widely appreciated. God, who is truth, has revealed Himself in His inspired, inerrant word – "Thy word is truth" (John 17:17). However, the essential connection between "*the local assembly* and truth", which will be the focus of this chapter, is not so well recognised.

The Pauline Metaphor Explained

The Bible's plainest statement on this vital subject appears in 1 Timothy 3:15, where the assembly is called the "pillar and ground of the truth". But what exactly does this mean?

A 'pillar' usually holds up some kind of structure. However, from ancient times, pillars have also served as objects to which public announcements can be affixed for all to see and read. This latter usage works well in this verse and helpfully distinguishes between the 'pillar' and the 'ground'. A 'ground' is a 'stay' or a 'base', upon which something can safely stand or lean. So, putting these two words 'pillar' and 'ground' together, a seventh purpose for the local assembly is revealed: *it exists to proclaim* (pillar) *and preserve* (ground) *divine truth.*

What is included under this word 'truth'? Jim Allen states, "The expression 'the truth' [in 1 Tim 3:15]…is not to be limited to any one aspect of truth. It is that which, revealed in Christ who is the truth, is maintained in a witness to Him. All aspects of absolute truth will thus be maintained as to His person and work (evangelically), as to His purpose and witness in this age (ecclesiastically), and to His promised return and kingdom (eschatologically)".[1] In other words, the local assembly is tasked with maintaining and bearing testimony to all of God's truth.

One looks in vain to the institutions of society – the government, academia, the judiciary and the press – to defend the truth of God. Even Christendom, despite its historic creeds, its grand synods and its theological seminaries, finds itself thoroughly permeated with every form of error and compromise. What then is God's vehicle, in the present dispensation, for the proclamation, preservation and transmission of His truth? The local assembly. No other entity has been designated 'pillar and ground of the truth'. Think of it: in a world of confusion, error and darkness, each local assembly, gathered to the Lord's name, is designed to be a divinely-planted beacon and bastion of truth.

The Historical Record Examined

The record of the New Testament gives evidence that the early Christians clearly understood and treasured this collective responsibility towards truth. On the day when local assembly testimony began we read this: "Then they that gladly **received** his word were **baptised**: and the same day there were **added** unto them about three thousand souls. And they **continued steadfastly** in **the apostles' doctrine** [that is the truth we have been thinking about] and **fellowship**, and in **breaking of bread**, and in **prayers**" (Acts 2:41-42, KJV).

The structure of these two verses revolves around 4 actions and 4 items, the order of which is deliberate and significant in each case.

The 4 actions establish a basic 'event order' that is to be repeated every time someone responds to the gospel. First, a person **receives** the message. Second, they are **baptised**. Third, they are **added** to an assembly. And fourth, they 'continue steadfastly'.

The next verse outlines the 4 items *in which* they continued steadfastly, each of which is preceded by a definite article

1. 'The' apostles' doctrine
2. 'The' fellowship
3. 'The' breaking of bread
4. 'The' prayers

Take careful notice of the first item. What does it mean to "continue steadfastly in the apostles' doctrine"? 'The apostles' doctrine', when Acts 2:42 was written, consisted of the verbal teaching being given by the 12 apostles. For us today, now that the Bible is complete, the apostles' doctrine is that full body of teaching, that sacred deposit of divine truth, called in Scripture "the faith...once for all delivered to the saints" (Jude v. 3, NKJV).

Each brother and sister in the first local assembly (in Acts 2) *persevered diligently in and adhered closely to Bible doctrine.* That's what "continuing steadfastly in the apostles' doctrine" means. Of course, that presupposes they were taught the truth, and grasped the truth, and cherished the truth. But just imagine, for a moment, such an assembly of 'committed and continuing' truth-lovers in first century Jerusalem. What was their character? They were "pillar and ground of the truth"! Is that how people perceive the assembly of which you form a part? Are you known as truth-lovers, truth-promoters and truth-defenders?

The Practical Ramifications Explored

It is not easy for an assembly to maintain its character as "pillar and ground of the truth". It will involve elders and other gifted brethren in constant Bible exposition and exhortation as they fulfil the task outlined in 2 Timothy 4:2: "Preach the word...reprove, rebuke, exhort with all longsuffering and doctrine". The local assembly should be a 'teaching centre' for the whole counsel of God, full of 'well-taught' believers who know what it is to "let the word of Christ dwell in you richly" (Col 3:16). An assembly starved of good teaching is unlikely to prosper. Paul was concerned that when the church came together everyone should 'learn', and all things should be "done to edification [building up]" (1 Cor 14:26). When young people go home from your local Bible Class or mid-week teaching meeting, are they saying to themselves, "I really learnt something today and felt the challenge of it"? They should be.

The four items in Acts 2:42 come in two pairs. The NKJV makes this clear: "And they continued steadfastly in the apostles' doctrine and fellowship [1st pair], in the breaking of bread and in prayers [2nd pair]".

The way the Bible pairs doctrine and fellowship together here is hugely significant. It indicates that the apostles' doctrine actually formed and informed the fellowship they enjoyed. The 'fellowship' in verse 42 is not the sharing of goods mentioned in verses 44-46. Here the fellowship

(Gk. *koinonos*) is their association and partnership in spiritual things – the oneness of spirit they enjoyed in assembly testimony.[2]

Many today tell us that "doctrine divides", and they recommend that all professing Christians set aside their doctrinal differences and 'unite in love'. But that is not what the Bible teaches. In Acts 2:42, fellowship was not a 'means to an end'. Fellowship was not something they agreed to have: it was something they had because they agreed; and their *theological unity* enabled them to have meaningful *practical unity*. And so it is today. *It is only when you have oneness in truth that you can work together to declare and defend that truth!*

So in actual fact, doctrine unites! It unites believers who share a love of the truth, and desire to continue steadfastly in it. Any attempt at 'fellowship' that compromises Bible doctrine on the person of Christ, salvation by faith alone, baptism by immersion, headship and the Lord's return, i.e. "the apostles' doctrine", is not Biblical fellowship.

If an assembly is to be the pillar and ground of the truth, it not only needs a healthy diet of year-round Bible teaching, but it also needs to maintain separation from error and false teachers (Rev 2:12-17). Paul likens false teaching to leaven [yeast] and warns that "a little leaven leaveneth the whole lump" (Gal 5:9). So assemblies need to be careful about who they receive into fellowship, and who they allow to teach. Remember, *fellowship with a man is fellowship with his doctrine*, and those who hold beliefs contrary to sound doctrine should be avoided (Rom 16:17).

How is this doctrinal fellowship expressed? That brings us to the second pair of items – "the breaking of bread" and "the prayers". These expressions refer to the Lord's Supper and the prayer meeting respectively. Our "continuing steadfastly" is therefore a two-pronged undertaking. It involves both what we believe, and what we practise – and these two should never be separated. So, for example, all those who participate in the activities of the breaking of bread and the assembly prayer meeting should wholeheartedly believe and hold to the apostles' doctrine.

One final point: truth should not only be declared and defended – it should be passed on to the next generation. Says the apostle Paul: "...the things that thou hast heard of me...*the same* commit thou to faithful men, who shall be able to teach others also" (2 Tim 2:1-2). May it be so, that after we are gone, the pillar will still be standing, the base unmoved!

---

[1] J. Allen, *What the Bible Teaches, 1 Timothy* (Kilmarnock, John Ritchie Ltd. 1983), p. 227

[2] It would be strange for Luke to introduce the idea of the distribution of financial fellowship in between "the apostles' doctrine" and "the breaking of bread and the prayers".

8

The Local Assembly Fulfils the Divine Commission

Our thoughts now turn to "the great commission" in which the Lord Jesus told His disciples to go into all the world and *preach* the gospel, *baptise* the converts, and *teach* them to observe all things that He had commanded. Having looked at the issue of *teaching* in chapter seven, we close this book with a look at *gospel preaching* and its relationship to the local assembly.

The New Testament is clear. *All evangelism is assembly-based*. That is to say, God has designated local assemblies – not para-church organisations, or committees, or 'ministries' – to be the vehicle for the fulfilling of 'the great commission'. That is the uniform record of the book of Acts and the epistles. Evangelists in the New Testament were not unaffiliated free agents! They were commended by and responsible to local assemblies.

Take Paul the apostle, for example. When he was called to preach the gospel, he was sent out *by the local assembly in Antioch* (Acts 13:3). He did not start "Paul Ministries Inc." and answer to a board of trustees! At the end of his first missionary journey he returned to his 'sending assembly' to report on all that God had done. Antioch is described as the place from which Paul and Barnabus "had been recommended to the grace of God for the work which they fulfilled" (Acts 14:26). This same principle applies to all believers engaged in evangelism – all gospel work must flow out from the local assembly and lead back to the assembly.

Christ's command to "preach the gospel" involves two major elements: first, preaching (**the method**), second, the gospel (**the message**).

Preaching

Many today want us to believe that preaching is outdated and ineffective. We are now told that the way to "reach the world for Christ" is through political involvement, social work and the performing arts. But what does the Bible say? "Go into all the word and *preach* the gospel". We wouldn't think of changing the message; so why change the method?

There are two chief proofs that 'preaching' is the prescribed method for communicating the gospel:

1. The Greek word for 'preach' used in 'the great commission'

The word the Lord used for 'preach' in Mark 16:15 means 'to herald' (Gk. *kerusso*). By using this particular word, He was indicating that evangelism is to be conducted first and foremost by public preaching.

2. How evangelism was conducted in the New Testament

The apostles clearly understood what Christ meant, because Peter, Paul, Philip and the other apostles all concentrated on and kept to *preaching*. Paul called himself a *preacher* (Gk. *kerux*, a herald) and asked "How shall they hear without one who *preaches*" (2 Tim 1:11, Rom 10:14).

But why did Christ send the 12 apostles into a first century culture saturated with politics, entertainment and drama, and tell them simply to *preach*? Because public preaching was, is and always will be the best and most suitable method for communicating gospel truth. How so? Because, in preaching, the Word of God is in full unobscured view; the spirit of the message is conveyed directly (eye to eye); the rational mind and conscience are engaged, and the tone of the method fits the content of the message.

So, assemblies are to send forth men of God, filled with the Spirit of God, to engage in the unobscured, direct and serious public heralding of the Word of God, aimed at the mind and conscience of sinners. The performing arts – acting, clowns, rock music, dance and puppets – represent a totally different genre of communication, wholly unsuited to the communication of the glorious gospel of our Lord Jesus Christ.

But what about the use of tracts, personal one-on-one witnessing, and other verbal and written presentations of the gospel? All of these are perfectly in order. They are subsets of preaching, aimed at the mind and conscience of the sinner. But they are not substitutes for preaching. Preaching must always be the main thing. It is what God has chosen and authorised, and it has been singularly blessed by God throughout history.

Is the assembly of which you form a part busy in gospel labour? Does it have a dedicated gospel meeting each week? Does it preach in the streets and markets of your area? Does it have regular concentrated series of consecutive daily gospel meetings? Is it a gospel-focussed, gospel-supporting assembly led by gospel-minded overseers? W.W. Fereday writing in the early 1900s remarked: "Sometimes it happens that the saints who are the best fed are the poorest workers. They would prefer endless Bible Readings to a vigorous gospel series". What a tragedy!

Message

The message we are to preach contains three essential elements. Man's **ruin** in sin, God's **remedy** in Christ, and man's **responsibility** to repent and believe the gospel. These elements are set forth in the great commission itself (see Luke 24:46-47 and Mark 16:16), as well as in the Roman epistle, which expounds the doctrine of the gospel.

Why start with man's ruin? Because a person must learn that they are guilty before they can be justified; that they are lost before they can be saved; that they are bound for hell before they can start for heaven!

And their problem is not just what they have done, but what they are. An awakening to their miserable and sinful condition by nature and practice is the proper backdrop for the good news of the gospel – that God so loved the world, that Christ died for the ungodly, and that God offers salvation as a free gift to bankrupt helpless sinners.

In preaching we must labour to convince our hearers that their nature is so corrupt that only the new birth can ever change them; that their guilt is so absolute that only a righteousness from God can ever fit them for heaven; that their sins are so vile that only the blood of Christ can cleanse them; and that their helplessness is so complete that only the mighty Victor of Calvary can ever deliver them.

What a privilege to be able to point sinners to the person and work of Christ, to tell them of His finished work and urge them to repent and believe the gospel. To press upon them their need to agree with what God says about their guilt and ruin, and receive the mercy which comes to them in that very condition! The sinner can do nothing, save to rest on what Another has done in his place. Taking God at His word he learns: "He was wounded...I am healed" (Isa 53:5). What a message!

Conclusion

We have seen that the local assembly is the only place on earth, in the present dispensation, where the Lord is present among His people; where His rule is acknowledged; where His order of headship is symbolically displayed, and where the Lord's Supper can be commemorated in remembrance of Him. It is the only entity designated "pillar and ground of the truth" and the only scriptural locus of operation for the carrying out of "the great commission".

Do you appreciate what it is to be part of an assembly? Are you prayerfully, intelligently and energetically contributing to its welfare? Do you understand that to be in God's assembly is, outside of the blessings of salvation, the greatest privilege a believer can enjoy?

One man who firmly grasped the uniqueness and significance of the assembly was the writer and Greek and Hebrew scholar, William Kelly, who graduated from Trinity College, Dublin, with first class distinction in highest classical honours. When, at the age of 23, he discovered the Bible's teaching about the function, character and pattern of the assembly, he gave up what he once thought would be a glittering career in 'the Church' and associated himself with other believers who shared his convictions. Many years later, writing a personal letter to a friend on 6th April 1902, he described the day he first gathered to break bread in New Testament simplicity, outside the traditions and systems of Christendom: *"I myself, when I left the English Establishment near 60 years ago, met two or three in a room of a private house – not larger than you and others have – and even then I felt it a privilege far beyond St Paul's or Westminster Abbey."*

May God lead each reader to be able to say of the assembly what Jacob said of Bethel; "Surely the LORD is in this place...How dreadful [awesome] is this place! This is none other but the house of God, and this is the gate of heaven" (Gen 28:16-17). May the Lord be pleased to teach us more of His blessed ways, to appreciate the place of His name, and to love "the habitation of Thy house, the place where Thine honour dwelleth" (Psa 26:8).

Acknowledgements

Many thanks to Phil Coulson for the suggestion to turn a single sermon into a series of articles for the Believer's Magazine.

Thanks also to John Ritchie Ltd. for now publishing the articles in book form, thus making the contents more widely available and more easily accessible.

My gratitude also to Bob Berry for his meticulous work in improving my grammar and punctuation.

Sincere thanks is also due to those faithful Bible teachers from whom I first learned many of these truths in my youth, notably Willie Trew, Jack Hunter, Norman Crawford and Jim Allen, among others.

Recommended Books for Further Reading

New Testament Church Principles by Arthur G. Clarke
John Ritchie Ltd., Kilmarnock, Scotland. 1992. 123 pages. 9780946351343

Some Scriptural Principles of the Christian Assembly by Henry Hitchman
Gospel Tract Publications, Glasgow, Scotland. 1988. 202 pages

The Glory of the Local Church by various authors
Assembly Testimony, Belfast, N.I., 2008. 222 pages.

The Church of God – Its Truth and Principles by Franklin Ferguson
Amainthakarai Gospel Hall, Chennai, India. 1999. 170 pages.

There Am I by Mark Sweetnam
Scripture Teaching Library, Cookstown, N.I., 2015. 99 pages.
9781909789302

New Testament Symbols by Alan Summers
John Ritchie Ltd., Kilmarnock, Scotland. 44 pages. 9781910513323

Reception to God's Assembly by William Bunting
John Ritchie Ltd., Kilmarnock, Scotland. 1933. 48 pages. 9780946351336

Church Doctrine and Practice by various authors
(edited by John Heading and Cyril Hocking)
Precious Seed Publications, Sheffield, England. 1971. 336 pages.
9781871642131